CULTURE IN ACTION

Photography

Liz Miles

www.raintreepublishers.co.uk
Visit our website to find out more information about Raintree books.

To order:
☎ Phone +44 (0) 1865 888066
🖨 Fax +44 (0) 1865 314091
💻 Visit www.raintreepublishers.co.uk

Raintree is an imprint of Capstone Global Library Limited, a company incorporated in England and Wales having its registered office at 7 Pilgrim Street, London, EC4V 6LB – Registered company number: 6695582

"Raintree" is a registered trademark of Pearson Education Limited, under licence to Capstone Global Library Limited

Text © Capstone Global Library Limited 2010
First published in hardback in 2010

Edited by Louise Galpine, Rachel Howells, and Helen Cox
Designed by Kimberly Miracle and Betsy Wernert
Original illustrations © Capstone Global Library Ltd.
Illustrated by kja-artists.com and Medi-mation (p. 16)
Picture research by Hannah Taylor and Kay Altwegg
Production by Alison Parsons
Originated by Dot Gradations Ltd.
Printed in China by CTPS.

ISBN 978 1 406212 06 8
14 13 12 11 10
10 9 8 7 6 5 4 3 2 1

British Library Cataloguing in Publication Data
Miles, Elizabeth
Photography. – (Culture in action)
770
A full catalogue record for this book is available from the British Library.

Acknowledgements
We would like to thank the following for permission to reproduce photographs: Alamy pp. **16 top** (© vanneilbob), **18** (© I. Glory), **20** (© vario images GmbH & Co.KG); ©Andy Goldsworthy p. **5**; ©Capstone Publishers pp. **17, L-R, 22**, and **23, top to bottom** (Karon Dubke); Corbis pp. **24** (Frans Lanting), **28** (Leo Mason); Getty Images pp. **19** (Time Life Pictures/ National Archives/ Ansel Adams), **25** (Hulton Archive/ Ernst Haas), **26** (David McNew), **29** (Time Life Pictures/ Jeffrey L. Rotman); PA Photos pp. **4** (DPA), **12** (Gareth Copley), **21** (AP Photo/Nick Ut); Science & Society Picture Library pp. **6** (Science Museum), **7, 8, 9**, and **10** (National Media Museum).

Icon and banner images supplied by Shutterstock: © Alexander Lukin, © ornitopter, © Colorlife, and © David S. Rose.

Cover photograph of sneaky photographer getting his shot, reproduced with permission of istockphoto (© PeskyMonkey).

We would like to thank Brian Payne, Jackie Murphy, and Nancy Harris for their invaluable help in the preparation of this book.

Contents

Photographs all around us   4

Camera beginnings   6

How do cameras work?   12

In the darkroom   18

From camera to newsroom   20

Digital camera controls   22

The perfect photograph   24

Far out photography   28

Glossary   30

Find out more   31

Index   32

Some words are printed in bold, **like this**. You can find out what they mean by looking in the glossary on page 30.

Photographs all around us

Photographs are everywhere – newspapers, magazines, books, postcards, and **galleries**. A photographer has taken every photograph you see. A photographer has looked through a camera, and pressed the button.

What's in a photograph?

Anything can be in a photograph. Newspaper photographs range from lively shots of smiling celebrities to horrific pictures of war scenes. Book and magazine photographs show lots of things, from fossils to fish, and cakes to castles.

Every photographer wants to take the best photograph of famous people such as Lewis Hamilton. It is a very competitive business.

Medical staff take different kinds of photographs. They take x-rays to photograph **organs** and bones in the body. Astronomers use telescopes to photograph the stars in outer space. Artists take photographs of their art, such as sculptures. Artistic photographs are displayed in **galleries**, like paintings.

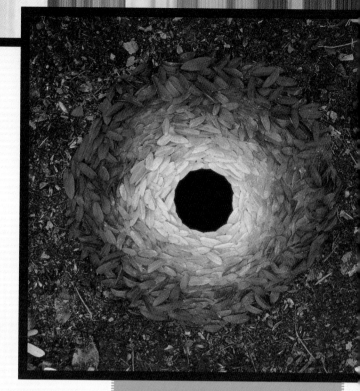

The artist Andy Goldsworthy took this photograph of his outdoor sculpture, called *Rowan Leaves and Hole*. The sculpture of leaves will not last forever, but the photograph will.

An exciting life

Professional photographers have to take really good photographs every day to earn a living. **Amateur** photographers can have fun taking **snapshots** of their families and friends. Others take their hobby more seriously. They practise hard and win competitions.

Multi-skilled

Photographers need many skills. They need to have an artistic eye. This means they have to be able to see what makes an attractive photograph, or a good **composition**. They also need to know how to use a camera. There are other important tools, too, such as **lenses**, lighting equipment, and computers. A lens sharpens the image.

Greek origins

The word "photography" comes from the Greek words *photos*, which means light, and *graphos*, which means writing.

Camera beginnings

A picture is a lasting reminder of an event or person. For thousands of years, the only pictures people had were drawings, paintings, **prints** (paper images), or carvings. In 1824, this changed when the world's first photograph was taken.

Camera obscura

In the 4th and 5th centuries, people started to find out how to make pictures. They noticed that if light passed through a pinhole into a darkened room, it made an upside-down image on the opposite wall. By the 1500s, **portable**, box-shaped versions of these rooms were made. They were called camera obscuras. These cameras were portable and had a pinhole on one side.

During the 1500s, a **lens** and mirror were put in camera obscuras. The lens made the image clearer. The mirror reflected (shone) the image out of the box onto the top. This made it easier to see. Also, people could now trace the image to make a drawing.

This camera obscura is from the early 1700s.

The first photograph

In 1826, French inventor Joseph Niépce came up with a new idea. He covered a piece of coated metal plate with soft tar and put it in the back of a camera obscura. He used the lens to shine an image onto it. The tar hardened into the image. It was the first real photograph. The fuzzy photograph showed a pigeon house and barn.

Capturing light

Photographs are made by capturing light on a **light-sensitive** surface. Today, the light-sensitive surface can be film or an electronic device.

Daguerreotype

Another French inventor, Louis Daguerre, improved Niépce's method. Daguerre's photographs were more detailed. They usually showed portraits of people. These photographs were called daguerreotypes. But there was still only one copy of each image.

This is the oldest surviving daguerreotype photograph, made in 1837.

From positive to negative

In the 1830s English inventor William Henry Fox Talbot was the first to take **negative** images. These are pictures with the light and dark tones reversed. The negatives were very useful. Each negative could be made into more than one **positive print** of each image. This meant that the light and dark tones were not reversed. Lots of copies (prints) of one photograph could be made. It also meant that photographs could appear in newspapers, books, and magazines for the first time!

The term

Astronomer Sir John Herschel called Talbot's invention of printing positive images from a negative "photography". It was a term that stuck!

In Victorian times you had to keep still for 30 seconds or more to have a photograph taken.

Wet and dry plates

Until the 1870s, photographic **plates** were "wet". They were sticky and coated in **chemicals**. Photographers had to carry round the plates and chemicals, as well as their big cameras. The plates had to be **developed** (made into photographs) within 10 minutes of the image being taken. So photographers had to travel around with their own **darkroom**. This was a place where a photograph could be developed. In 1871, "dry plates" were made. These were less messy, easier to use, and did not have to be developed right away.

The first colour photograph ever taken was of a tartan ribbon.

Colour

For many years people tried, but failed, to take colour photographs. So black and white photographs were often touched up or painted with watercolours or inks. The first plates that took colour photographs were made in 1907. Modern colour films were first sold in 1935. They were called Kodachrome.

Anyone could take a **snapshot** with a Kodak Brownie.

Photographic film

In 1884, **photographic film** was invented. It is a **light-sensitive** paper that records images. It replaced heavy plates and could be rolled up to fit into smaller cameras.

In 1888, the first camera with rolled film went on sale. The buyers were told, "You press the button, we do the rest". The buyer could take their photographs, then send the film to be developed. Taking photographs was easier, and people did not have to keep still for ages to have their photograph taken.

At first, these cameras were too expensive for most people to buy. Then, in 1900, the first cheaper camera went on sale – the Kodak Brownie. It was an instant success.

Camera technology quickly improved. Electronic **flash** was introduced in 1931 to lighten photographs, for example. The first **digital camera** went on sale in 1990. Fourteen years later, digital cameras were more popular than film cameras.

Match the mood

What's in a photograph? Of course, there is the **subject** (such as a person or a view), but there will also be a mood. The aim of this activity is to find music to match the mood of each of your photographs.

You will need:

• A selection of old photographs (black and white if possible)

• A newspaper and scissors

• Various CDs of different types of music (classical and pop, if possible).

Steps to follow:

1. Choose a photograph from your selection, or cut out a photograph from a newspaper.

2. Play two or three different pieces of music as you look at the photograph. Does the different music make you spot details in the photograph? Does quiet music show up how a shy person is looking away? Does loud music make you notice a dark cloud in the sky?

3. Decide on the main mood of the photograph. Match a piece of music to it.

4. Write a title for the photograph to fit its mood.

5. Show your photograph to a friend. Play the music you chose. Can your friend think of any other music that could go with your photograph?

How do cameras work?

The body of a camera is like a lightproof box – a sealed box that light cannot get into. When the button is pressed to take a picture, the shutter (a kind of door) opens for less than a second. This lets light from the **subject** pass through a hole (the **aperture**) into the camera. A **lens** focuses the image onto the **light-sensitive** film at the back.

Some useful definitions

Depth of field – the area (part) of an image that is in focus

Focus – to make a photograph clear and un-fuzzy. Turning the camera lens does this.

Focal length – the distance from the centre of a lens to its focal point. This is the point at which the image of a distant object is in focus.

A fast shutter speed on a camera allows a photographer to take a split-second image of a fast-moving object.

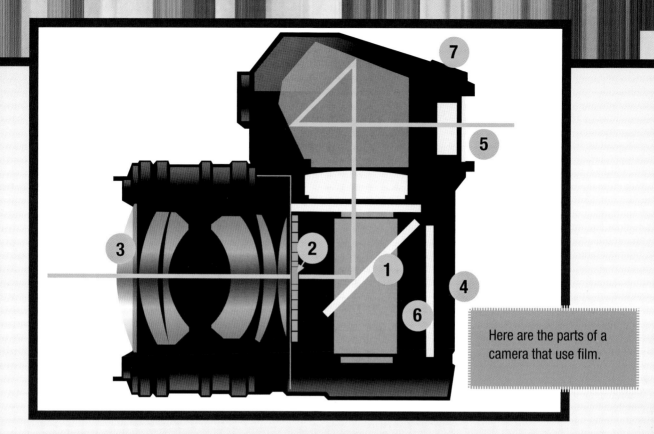

Here are the parts of a camera that use film.

1. *Mirror:* A piece of glass that reflects light that comes through the lens, and allows you to see the image through the **viewfinder**.

2. *Aperture:* A ring around the aperture can be widened or narrowed. This controls the **exposure** (how much light gets in).

3. *Lens:* A camera lens is made up of a series of pieces of glass. Turning the lens can sharpen or blur the image. The lens controls how far you can zoom in or out on the image. Lenses can focus on something close to the camera, or something far away.

4. *Film:* What you put in the camera to take a photograph. It usually comes in a roll. After you take the picture you move the film on. This allows you to take another photograph on the same roll.

5. *Viewfinder:* Small opening to look through. You can see what you're photographing.

6. *Shutter:* This works like a window and only opens when you push the shutter button on your camera. When the shutter opens, this allows the image you see through the viewfinder to be captured on the roll of film.

7. *Shutter button:* When you press the shutter button this opens and closes the shutter, and takes the photograph.

Do you see what the camera sees?

When you look through the **viewfinder** of certain types of cameras, you see exactly the same image as goes through the lens. This image will be on the film and printed photograph. To get a perfect photograph, it is better to see the photograph you are taking. You need to see what the camera sees.

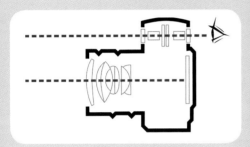

Viewfinder camera

The viewfinder is at the top, so you look through the top of the camera. But the light from the image passes through the lens, which is lower down. You do not see what the camera sees.

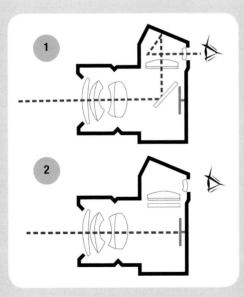

Single reflex camera

Even though the viewfinder is above the lens, you still see the image that is coming through the lens, right up to the second the picture is taken. A mirror reflects the light of the image up to a glass block and into the viewfinder (picture 1). When you press the button to take the picture, the mirror flips up. Light then passes to the film (picture 2).

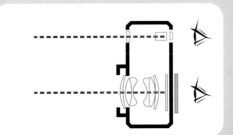

Digital camera

You will see what the camera sees if the digital camera has an **LCD screen**. An LCD screen is a large screen on the back of the camera.

How does a digital camera work?

Like film cameras, **digital cameras** have a body, a shutter, and a lens. But digital cameras do not capture an image on a roll of film.

Digital cameras capture the image on a **light sensor**. The sensor picks up the patterns of light from the image. The patterns of light are changed into **digital signals**. The signals are stored in the camera on a tiny **memory card**.

Pixels

Digital photographs are made up of millions of squares of colour (called **pixels**). The more pixels there are, the sharper the picture. Usually 200 pixels per inch is enough for a good **print**.

From camera to printer

Computers and printers can "read" the digital signals on a memory card and turn them into images. How do you get the images from the camera to a computer or printer? To do this the memory card is taken from the camera and plugged into the computer or printer. It is also possible to pass the images down a cable, from camera to computer.

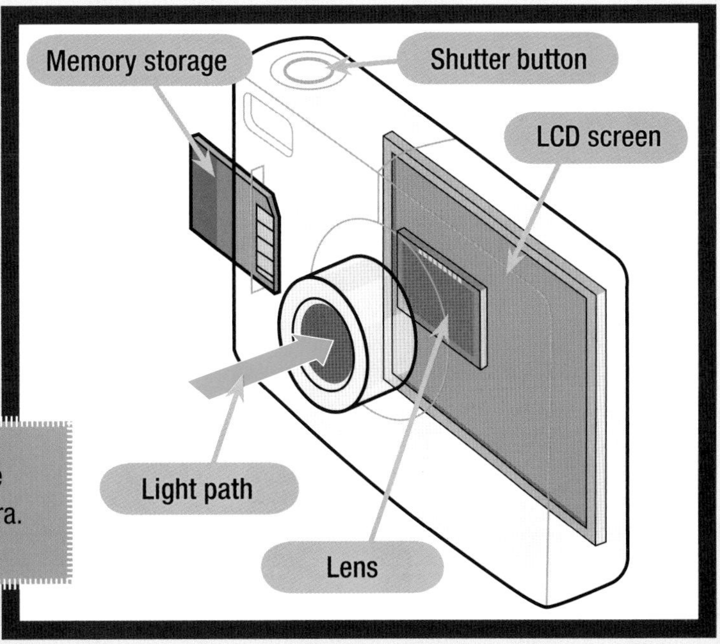

This diagram shows the inside of a digital camera.

Memory storage

Shutter button

LCD screen

Light path

Lens

Depth of field

If you take a photograph of a crowded beach, only a part of the scene will look sharp. This area is called the depth of field. To get a bigger depth of field (so that more of the picture is in focus), photographers make the camera's **aperture** smaller. Another way is to change the lens.

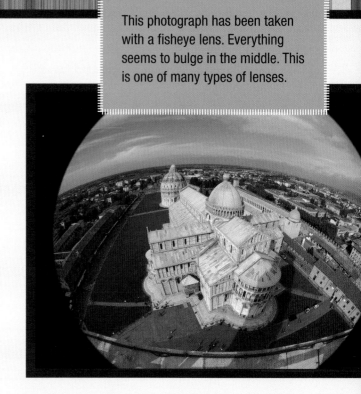

Filter and flash

White light is made up of all the colours seen in a rainbow. Filters can block out some of the colours to make bolder colours, such as a very blue sky.

A **flash** makes extra light. People often use their camera's flash indoors and at night. However, it can also be useful to lighten shadowy areas in daytime shots.

A camera lens gathers light rays from outside and focuses them into an image on the camera's film or sensor.

Fashion shoots and mug shots

Fashion shoot

Work with a friend on a fashion photo shoot.

You will need:

- Some interesting-looking clothes
- A digital camera

Steps to follow:

1. Find a well-lit room. You may need to use the flash on the camera.

2. The photographer should guide the model on the best poses to show off the clothes.

3. Take photographs from different angles and distances.

4. Print the photographs.

5. Make a page for a fashion magazine. Write captions and an article describing the clothing.

How to take people photographs:

- check the person is relaxed
- don't always insist on a smile (there's nothing worse than a false grin)
- check the pose – make sure the person's hands are relaxed
- find a good setting
- experiment with props (capture the person doing an activity such as painting).

Mug shots

Work with a friend to make a sequence of portraits. The model should show a different emotion for each shot. Can your friends guess the emotion?

A happy face | A confused face | A sad face | A surprised face

In the darkroom

Many good photographers **develop** and print their own photographs. The processes are described below. They take place in a **darkroom**, where there is no natural light. Daylight would ruin the **light-sensitive** equipment.

From camera to gallery

1. In complete darkness, the film is taken out of the camera.

2. It is put in a developing tank.

3. **Chemicals** are added, and then tipped out, one at a time.

4. The film is washed and hung to dry. The developed film is called a **negative**. This is because the dark and light tones are reversed.

5. Next, the printing process begins. The negative is put in an enlarger. This beams a larger, sharper version of each image on to a sheet of light-sensitive paper.

6. The paper (now called a **print**) is put in a chemical. Gradually, the image appears.

7. It is put in other chemicals, rinsed, and hung to dry.

Some darkrooms are lit with a safe light. A safe light is a red or orange light that does not spoil the paper used for printing black and white photographs.

Amazing black and whites

Black and white photographs are often more impressive than colour. The shapes and shadows stand out. The contrast between black shadows and white highlights is dramatic.

Here is *Tetons and Snake River* by the American photographer, Ansel Adams.

Ansel Adams

Photographer Ansel Adams (1902–84) knew there was more to taking a photograph than pressing a button. He once said, "You don't take a photograph, you make it."

From camera to newsroom

A photograph can be taken, processed, and printed within minutes. But this is only possible with the help of a **digital camera** and computers. **Photojournalists** use them to get up-to-the-minute photographs to newspaper offices.

From camera to newspaper

If there is an earthquake somewhere in the world, photojournalists rush to get up-to-date photographs to their newspaper editors. Here is a typical timeline of what might happen:

1:00 p.m. – earthquake in Indonesia

2:00 p.m. – photojournalist arrives at damaged village and takes photographs

2:10 p.m. – uploads photographs to a laptop

2:11 p.m. – sends photographs by satellite to the newspaper office in London

2:13 p.m. – photographs received and passed to picture department

2:30 p.m. – photograph selected and edited on computer

2:35 p.m. – photograph sent to printers for front page of newspaper

5:00 p.m. – evening edition of newspaper on sale.

A laptop and satellite dish transmits photographs to the other side of the world in seconds.

Photographs may need to be cropped to fit a space on a newspaper page.

Photograph editing

You can change a photograph completely using a computer and photo-editing program. Colours can be altered, people deleted, objects added, and so on. In photojournalism, the editing is usually quite subtle. For example, sections may be cropped, or cut off.

You decide

Should photographs for newspapers be manipulated at all? Here are some different views.

Yes:
- newspapers need good photographs so people will buy them
- photographs are like paintings, there is nothing wrong with improving them.

No:
- photographs should tell the truth — they should be exactly what the photographer saw
- if we change some photographs, we can't believe anything we see.

Digital camera controls

Digital cameras are very popular. They are easy to use but lots of people never find out all that they can do. The controls shown here are some of the most useful ones. The controls and symbols on other models may be different. To make the most of your camera, read the instruction booklet.

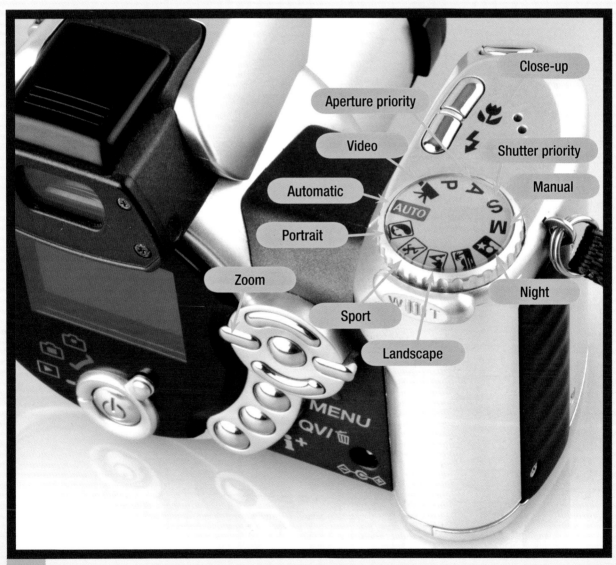

Close-up

Aperture priority

Video

Shutter priority

Automatic

Manual

Portrait

Zoom

Night

Sport

Landscape

Aperture priority: Set the **aperture** you want (on a bright day, a smaller aperture will let in less light; on a darker day, a larger aperture will let in more light).

Automatic: The camera sorts out the **flash** and focus for you. All you do is point and click!

Close-up: Use this if the **subject** is closer than about 60 centimetres.

Landscape: Use this for distant subjects, such as landscapes – just like the mountains in the symbol.

Manual: For when you want to take control of the **exposure**.

Night: For night-time photographs, or for when the subject is in dark shadows.

Portrait: For people or head-and-shoulder shots, when the background isn't important.

Shutter priority: Set the shutter speed you want (use a slower shutter speed for darker days, but use a fast shutter speed for moving objects or they will look blurred).

Sport: This is not just for fast-moving sports – use it for any moving objects, such as birds or cars.

Video: For taking a short video-clip.

Zoom: This will operate the zoom **lens** (if you have one). Use it for getting closer to your **subject**.

Picture with zoom

Picture without zoom

Overexposure

Portrait

Shutter priority

23

The perfect photograph

How do you take a good photograph? Firstly, it is important to learn to use your own camera. Read the instructions and get to know how to use the controls. Secondly, choose your **subject** carefully.

Composition

Photography is an art and some photographs are hung in **galleries**. Like paintings, they should show interesting colours, lines, and shapes.

To compose a photograph you must decide where to position different parts. Avoid putting your subject in the centre. If it is a third of the way down from the top or a third of the way up, it will be much more interesting. This is known as the "rule of thirds".

This photograph of a zebra in Africa is by Frans Lanting.

Focal point

Every photograph must have a focal point – the part that draws the viewer's eye. Make sure it is uncluttered by an over-busy background.

Ernst Haas

This Austrian photographer is well known for his use of colour and experiments with light. He called himself "a painter in a hurry". This photograph shows the lights of Tokyo, Japan, reflected in a wet street.

Ernst Haas took this photograph during his travels in Japan in 1984.

Frans Lanting

This Dutch nature photographer works hard to get close enough to wild animals to take amazing photographs. In the photograph on page 24, he has used the rule of thirds in placing his subject a third of the way down the photograph. There is also nothing to distract you from the focal point.

Light

Outdoors, if you want your subject fully lit, check that the sun is behind you. Taking a photograph into the sun can cause problems, unless you have a filter. Sunlight from the side can cast interesting shadows. Dramatic weather can cause interesting light and shadows, too. Indoor photographs can use natural light from a large window. This gives a softer light than the harsh, direct light of a **flash**.

Choose your moment

Light and shadows change during the day. Try taking the same image, such as a tree, from the same place early morning, mid morning, at midday, and at sunset. The varying light will affect the colours and shadows and you will end up with four very different photographs.

Annie Leibovitz

Lots of photographers have become famous for portraits. American photographer, Annie Leibovitz, takes portraits of celebrities. She uses complex lighting, such as flash outdoors.

Annie Leibovitz finds a good spot to photograph the new American President, Barack Obama, in Washington, DC, 2009.

ART ACTIVITY

Gallery shot

Still life paintings have been popular since the 1600s. They are paintings of carefully placed objects. Usually the objects are inanimate (not alive or moving). This activity challenges you to compose a still life photograph using objects from the past.

Steps to follow:

1. Gather some objects from a specific time in history, such as the Victorian period, the 1960s, or perhaps the time when you were born. You could include clothes, jewellery, ornaments, toys, or even pictures.

2. Choose the most interesting objects from your selection, and try them alongside each other. Look through your camera and keep adjusting the objects to get the **composition** you want.

3. When you are happy, take several photographs from different angles and distances.

4. Get **prints** of your favourite shots.

5. Show your photographs to your friends. Can they guess how old the objects are?

Some tips

- Don't forget to choose the focal point. One or two items should stand out.
- Flash is not always necessary if you are working inside – light from a window can be very effective.
- If you have a computer and photo editing software available, try cropping your favourite photograph.

Far out photography

Photographers work all around the world, taking photographs of people, places, animals, and events. Astronauts take photographs in space. Controllers on the ground use cameras on satellites (spaceships that orbit Earth) to take photographs of distant planets, stars, and galaxies.

Photographers often work in dangerous or upsetting conditions. They have to take photographs in war zones, in the shadow of erupting volcanoes, or in areas where there are dangerous animals nearby.

Sports photographer Leo Mason captured this elegant jump by three gymnasts at the Beijing Olympics in 2008.

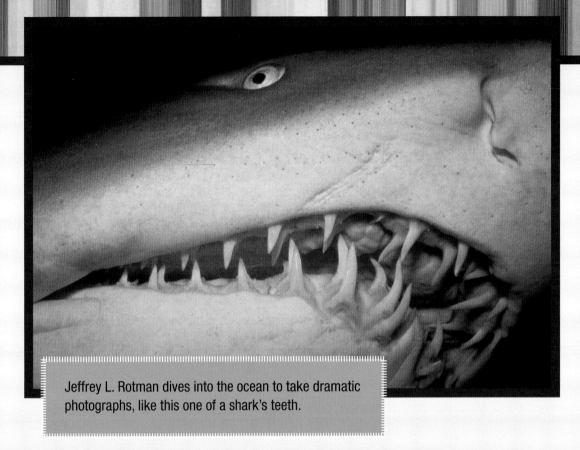

Jeffrey L. Rotman dives into the ocean to take dramatic photographs, like this one of a shark's teeth.

Photographers often have a mission. It could be helping to sell a product or pointing out an injustice (unfairness) in the world. Wildlife photographers show us rare animals, and remind us to help protect the natural world.

Photography jobs

What kind of photographer would you choose to be, and why? Which do the most important or interesting jobs? Discuss this question with your friends. Here are a few different types of photographer, and the things they try to do:

- Wildlife photographers – show animals that are in danger of extinction
- Fashion photographers – show the beauty of people and clothes, and help to sell clothes
- Art photographers – help people see beauty in the world, or to look at the world with a more critical eye
- **Photojournalists** – tell real-life stories, and reveal injustice in the world.

Glossary

amateur person who does something for fun, or as a hobby

aperture hole in a camera the size of a pin, through which light enters

chemical substance made up of atoms and molecules

composition what you include in a photograph and how you arrange things in a photograph

darkroom room where photographs are developed and printed

develop processing a film so that the images on it can be printed

digital camera camera that takes and stores images digitally

digital signal information in the form of numbers, that computers understand

exposure amount of light that is allowed to enter a camera and be recorded on the film or light sensor

flash bright light that flashes on a camera, to lighten the photograph

gallery building where art, including photographs, is shown

LCD screen large screen at the back of a digital camera

lens glass that sharpens an image

light-sensitive picks up light. The films in cameras are light-sensitive.

light sensor part of a digital camera that detects light and sorts it into an image

memory card card that goes in a digital camera, which photographs are saved to

negative image in which the colours are reversed, so black areas look white

organ part of the body that has a particular function

photographic film paper that picks up light when a camera takes a photograph

photojournalist professional photographer who takes news images

pixel squares of colour that make up digital photographs

plate hard sheet on which photographic images can be recorded

portable if an object is portable it means it can be carried around

positive image in which the colours are not reversed

print image that has been printed onto paper

professional someone who makes money selling the photographs they take

snapshot photographs that have been taken quickly, without much planning

subject person or object in a photograph

tripod stand with three legs, used to support a camera

viewfinder part of the camera you look through

Find out more

Books

Digital Photo Madness!: 50 Weird and Wacky Things to Do with Your Digital Camera, Thom Gaines (Lark Books, 2006)

Digital Photo Magic (Dorling Kindersley, 2008)

Photography (*What is Art?*), Karen Hosack (Raintree, 2008)

Websites

http://licm.org.uk/livingImage/CameraObscura.html
Find out how to make your own camera obscura.

http://animals.nationalgeographic.com/animals
This site has some amazing wildlife photography.

Famous photographer websites:

www.anseladams.com
Ansel Adams (black and white)

www.leomason.com
Leo Mason (sport)

www.stephendalton.co.uk
Stephen Dalton (animals)

Places to visit

The Kodak Gallery
National Media Museum
Bradford
West Yorkshire
BD1 1NQ
Tel: +44 (0) 1274 20 20 30
This permanent exhibition shows photography from the 1840s.

Index

Adams, Ansel 19
amateur photographers 5
aperture 12, 13, 16, 23
art photography 5, 24, 29
astronomy 5

black-and-white 19

cameras
    camera obscuras 6
    digital cameras 10, 14–15, 20, 22-23
    how cameras work 12–13
    single reflex camera 14
    viewfinder camera 14
celebrities 4, 26
close-ups 23
colour photography 9
composition 5, 24, 27
computers 15, 20, 21

Daguerre, Louis 7
daguerreotypes 7
darkrooms 9, 18
depth of field 12, 16
development 9, 18
digital cameras 10, 14–15, 20, 22–23
    controls 22-23
digital signals 15

exposure 13, 23

fashion 17, 29
film 10, 13
    rolled film 10
filters 16, 26
fisheye lens 16
flash 10, 16, 23, 26, 27
focal length 12
focal point 25, 27

focus 12, 16
Fox Talbot 8

Goldsworthy, Andy 5

Haas, Ernst 25
Herschel, Sir John 8

indoor photography 16, 26, 27

Kodachrome 9
Kodak Brownie 10

landscape 23
Lanting, Frans 24, 25
Leibovitz, Annie 26
lenses 5, 6, 12, 13, 15
    fisheye lens 16
    zoom lens 23
light and shadows 26
light capture 7, 15, 16
light-sensitive materials 7, 10, 12, 18
light sensors 15

Mason, Leo 28
medical photography 5
memory cards 15
mood 11
mug shots 17

negative images 8, 18
newspaper photography 20, 21, 29
Niépce, Joseph 7
night-time photos 16, 23

outdoor photography 26

photo-editing 21, 27
photographic plates 9

photography
    first photograph 7
    origin of the word 5, 8
    perfect photograph, taking the 24–25
    skills 5
photojournalists 20, 21, 29
pixels 15
portraits 17, 23, 26
positive images 8
prints 8, 15, 18
professional photographers 5
props 17

Rotman, Jeffrey L. 29
rule of thirds 24, 25

satellites 28
shutter 12, 13, 15
    shutter speed 12, 13, 23
single reflex camera 14
skills 5
snapshots 5, 10
space, photography in 5, 28
sports photography 12, 23, 28
still life photography 27
sunlight 26

tripod 25

video-clips 23
viewfinder 14

weather conditions 26
white light 16
wildlife photography 24, 25, 29

x-rays 5

zoom lens 23